CONSTELLATIONS
OF THE
NIGHT SKY

Bruce LaFo

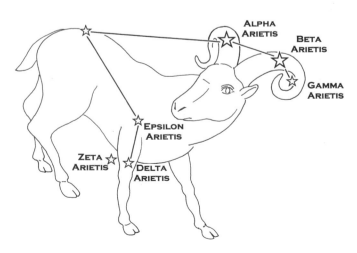

DOVER PUBLICATIONS, INC.
Mineola, New York

About the Author

BRUCE LAFONTAINE is the writer and illustrator of 42 non-fiction books for both children (ages 8-12) and adults. He specializes in books about history, science, transportation, and architecture. His published works include *Warriors Through the Ages, Great Inventors and Inventions, Famous Buildings of Frank Lloyd Wright*, and others. His book *Exploring the Solar System* (1999) was selected by *Astronomy* magazine as one of the twenty-one best astronomy books for children. He is included in *Something About the Author* and the *International Biographical Centre Who's Who of Authors*, hardcover publications profiling prominent authors and illustrators. He lives and works in the Rochester, New York area.

Bibliographical Note

Constellations of the Night Sky is a new work, first published by Dover Publications, Inc., in 2003.

DOVER *Pictorial Archive* SERIES

This book belongs to the Dover Pictorial Archive Series. You may use the designs and illustrations for graphics and crafts applications, free and without special permission, provided that you include no more than four in the same publication or project. (For permission for additional use, please write to Permissions Department, Dover Publications, Inc., 31 East 2nd Street, Mineola, N.Y. 11501.)

However, republication or reproduction of any illustration by any other graphic service, whether it be in a book or in any other design resource, is strictly prohibited.

International Standard Book Number: 0-486-42648-3

Manufactured in the United States of America
Dover Publications, Inc., 31 East 2nd Street, Mineola, N.Y. 11501

Introduction

Away from the lights of the city, the dark night sky offers an amazing and wondrous sight: thousands of brilliant, glittering stars. In fact, the name of one type of star, a *Mira variable*, comes from the Latin word for "wonderful." Because the ancient civilizations of Babylon, Egypt, Arabia, Greece, and Rome did not possess the scientific knowledge to understand the true nature of stars, they constructed elaborate myths and legends about the star formations they observed. We now call these star groups *constellations*. Although most of the myths are from ancient Greek lore, the names of the constellations have come down to us in the Roman language of Latin. And because of the achievements of ancient Arab astronomers, many individual star names are in Arabic.

Stars come in a variety of colors, sizes, and types. Among them are *red dwarfs*–twenty times smaller than our own Sun, and *supergiants*–100 times more massive. Stars also burn at different temperatures, indicated by their colors. Yellow-white stars like the Sun have surface temperatures of 5500 degrees centigrade, while blue-white and blue stars burn the hottest–30,000 to 60,000 degrees centigrade. Astronomers also measure stars according to their brightness. The brightness of a star is determined by two types of *magnitude*. Absolute magnitude refers to the brightness of a star in relation to other stars. Apparent magnitude, the scale used in this book, describes a star's brilliance as seen from Earth (see p. 48 for a list of the twenty-five brightest stars).

In addition to individual stars, constellations include other celestial configurations: double stars orbiting in close proximity around a central gravitational point; binary eclipsing variables, i.e., twin stars in which a smaller companion orbits a larger main star; and groups of stars called *clusters*. Globular clusters are tightly packed together, while others with less density are called "open" clusters. *Nebulae,* clouds of brightly shining gas and dust, are interstellar nurseries where newborn stars come winking into existence. The largest elements of constellations are huge accumulations of stars called *galaxies*. Some, like our own Milky Way galaxy, are spiral-shaped and contain over 200 billion stars.

Observed from Earth, stars and constellations change constantly. Their positions vary as they rise and set with the Earth's daily rotation on its own axis. The location of constellations also varies with the seasons. As the Earth moves along its yearly orbital path around the Sun, the natural tilt of the planet causes an apparent monthly change of constellation positions in the night sky. Moreover, some constellations are visible only in the Southern Hemisphere, below the equator. However, since most of the constellations in this book are visible from the Northern Hemisphere, the sky charts at the front and back show the generalized positions of major constellations in the Northern Hemisphere during summer and winter.

Wherever you live, this book will help you understand and appreciate the wonders of the heavens. Simply step outside on a clear, dark evening and discover the magnificent display of mythical animals, objects, and characters glowing brightly in the constellations of the night sky.

1. Aquarius
The Water Bearer

The constellation Aquarius is also known as "the water bearer." Aquarius is one of the oldest recognized groups of stars; observations have been recorded as far back as the Babylonians (ca. 1700 B.C.). The mythical Greek zodiac depiction shows a young man pouring water from the open mouth of a jar. Aquarius is associated with Zeus, King of the Gods, pouring the waters of life down to Earth from Mt. Olympus. A variation of the legend states that Zeus chose Ganymede, son of the King of Troy, to serve as Aquarius, the cupbearer to the gods on Mt. Olympus. In the zodiac, Aquarius is represented by the monthly time period from January 20 to February 18.

Aquarius is located in a region of the sky known in Babylonian myth as "the sea." Also included in this region are the constellations of Cetus (whale), Pisces (fish), Hydra (sea monster), and Capricorn (sea goat).

The brightest star in Aquarius is Sadalmelik (*Alpha Aquarii*), with a magnitude of 3.0. It is 945 light-years (the distance light travels in a year) from Earth. Other prominent celestial objects within Aquarius are the globular star cluster M2, the Saturn Nebula, and the Helix Nebula.

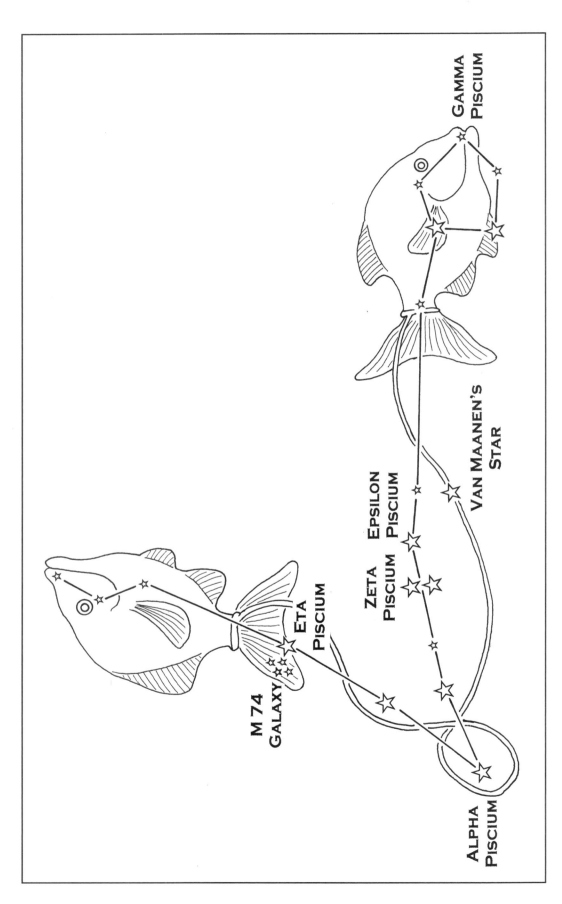

GAMMA PISCIUM

VAN MAANEN'S STAR

ZETA PISCIUM

EPSILON PISCIUM

ETA PISCIUM

M 74 GALAXY

ALPHA PISCIUM

2. Pisces
The Fish

The constellation Pisces is shown here as two fish bound together by a cord. This depiction is drawn from a Greek myth recounting how the goddess Aphrodite and her son Eros were driven into the sea by the monster Typhon. To rescue them, the sea god Poseidon sent two giant fish to carry them away. Zeus honored the fish by creating a new group of stars. The zodiac assigns Pisces the period from February 19 to March 20.

Although the constellation of Pisces is large, it contains no stars of great magnitude. Its brightest star, *Alpha Piscium*, is actually a *binary* star, two stars which orbit one another closely. They are located at the knot of the cord that binds the two fish and lie 140 light-years from Earth. The two stars have magnitudes of 4.2 and 5.2. Pisces also contains the spiral galaxy M74, and Van Maanen's Star, a rare *white dwarf* star.

3. Aries
The Ram

The constellation of Aries is represented by the Ram. The original Greek legend concerns the rescue of Phrixus and Helle, the son and daughter of the King of Thessaly, by a golden ram sent by the god Hermes (Mercury to the Romans). As the Ram was flying them to safety over the strait of water that separates Europe and Asia, Helle fell into the sea. In her honor, the Greeks named this body of water the Hellespont (Sea of Helle). Phrixus survived and was transported safely to the shores of the Black Sea. There, he sacrificed the golden ram to Hermes and placed its fleece under the protection of a dragon. This, in turn, gave rise to the legend of Jason and the Argonauts and their search for the Golden Fleece. Those with birthdays between March 21 and April 18 were born under the sign of Aries.

The constellation is mainly identified by three low-magnitude stars that symbolize the horns of the Ram. These are *Alpha, Beta,* and *Gamma Arietis* with magnitudes of 2.0, 2.6, and 4.6, respectively.

BETA ARIETIS

GAMMA ARIETIS

ALPHA ARIETIS

EPSILON ARIETIS

DELTA ARIETIS

ZETA ARIETIS

4. Taurus
The Bull

Containing a number of significant celestial objects, the constellation Taurus is one of the oldest star groups, its association with the bull dating back to the Chaldeans (3000 B.C.). The Greek myth tells the story of how Zeus transformed himself into a powerful white bull to catch the attention of Europa, the beautiful daughter of the King of Phoenicia. Entranced by the bull, she climbed on his back. He then carried her into the sea and swam to the Isle of Crete, where Europa later bore him a son, Minos. The time period of April 20 to May 20 is assigned to the constellation Taurus.

The brightest object in Taurus is the star Aldebaran, an *orange giant*. With a magnitude of 0.85 it is located sixty-eight light-years from Earth. It also contains two bright open star clusters, the Pleiades and the Hyades. The Pleiades is popularly known as the "Seven Sisters" after its seven principal stars, named for the daughters of Atlas. The Hyades is located at a relatively nearby 150 light-years from Earth. Also within Taurus is the M1 Crab Nebula, visible through a moderately powered telescope as an oval patch of light.

BETA TAURI

M 1 (CRAB NEBULA)

ZETA TAURI

PLEIADES STAR CLUSTER (SEVEN SISTERS)

HYADES STAR CLUSTER

ALDEBARAN (ALPHA TAURI)

LAMBDA TAURI

XI TAURI

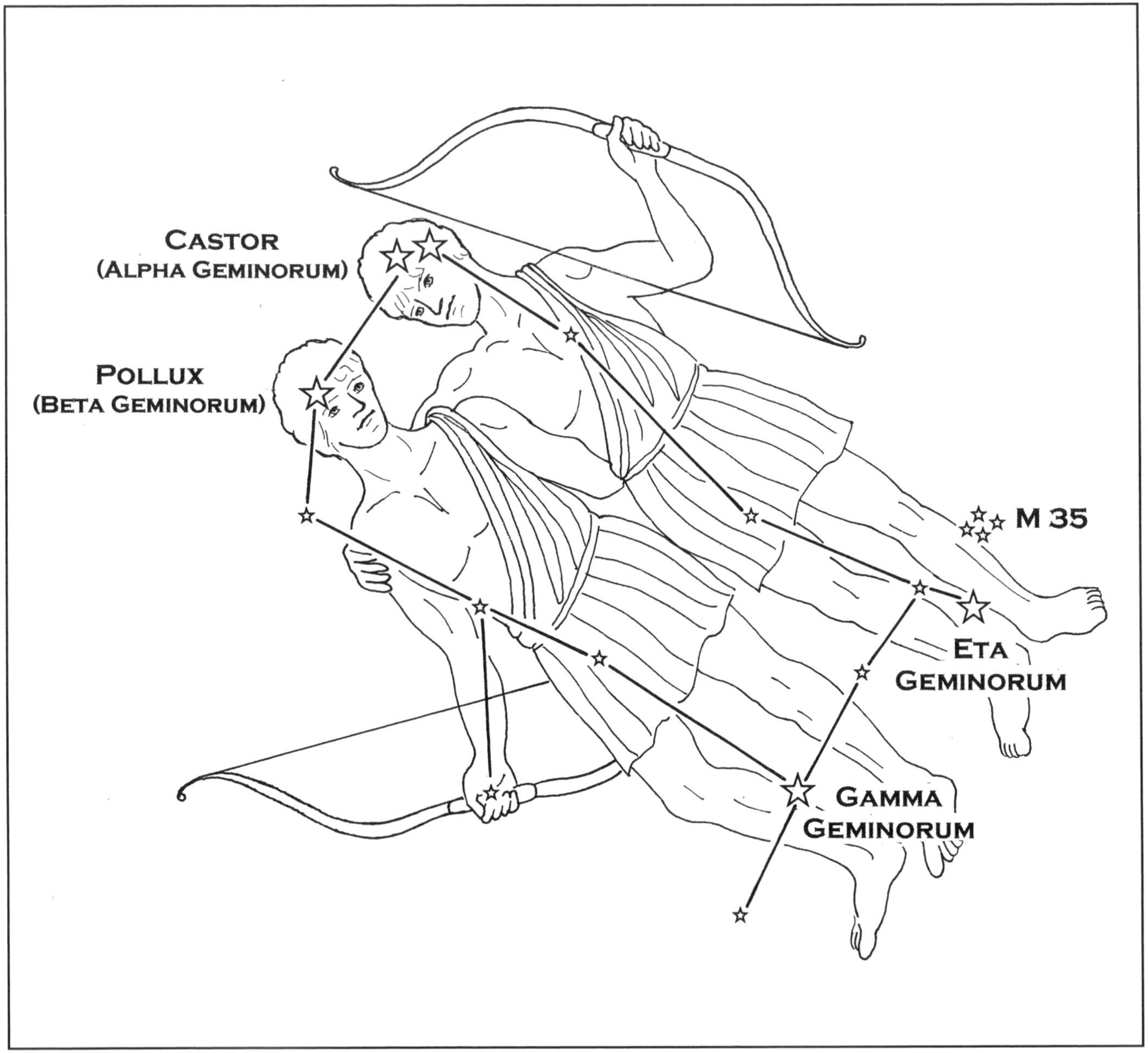

5. Gemini
The Twins

The constellation Gemini is based on the Greek myth of the twin brothers, Castor and Pollux. They were athletes and warriors who sailed with the legendary hero Jason on the great ship Argo, fighting at his side during many adventures. When Castor was killed, Pollux asked Zeus to let him die also so that he might be with his brother. Zeus granted his request, transforming the two brothers into nearby stars set forever in the night sky. The zodiac period given to Gemini is from May 21 to June 20.

The principal stars of Gemini are *Alpha Geminorum* (Castor), and *Beta Geminorum* (Pollux). Castor is a binary star with a combined magnitude of 1.6, while Pollux, the brightest star in Gemini, has a magnitude of 1.2. Also located within the constellation is the open star cluster M35.

CASTOR
(ALPHA GEMINORUM)

POLLUX
(BETA GEMINORUM)

M 35

ETA GEMINORUM

GAMMA GEMINORUM

6. Cancer
The Crab

The crab is the image associated with the constellation Cancer. The Greek myth is based on the exploits of the great hero Hercules. One of the twelve labors the gods of Olympus forced Hercules to perform was to defeat the sea monster Hydra, a pet of the goddess Hera. To help the Hydra in its battle with Hercules, Hera created a monstrous crab to seize the hero in its gigantic pincers. Using his enormous strength, Hercules crushed Cancer underfoot and killed the Hydra. The period from June 21 to July 22 is covered by Cancer.

The constellation contains the great star field known as M44, the Beehive Cluster (*Praesepe* in Latin). It is visible to the naked eye as a cloudy patch of light, but through binoculars, a large field of individual stars can be seen. The brightest star in Cancer is *Beta Cancri* with a magnitude of 3.5. The constellation also contains the star cluster M67, located a distant 2,600 light-years from Earth.

IOTA CANCRI

GAMMA CANCRI

DELTA CANCRI

M 44 PRAESEPE (BEEHIVE) STAR CLUSTER

ZETA CANCRI

M 67 STAR CLUSTER

ALPHA CANCRI

BETA CANCRI

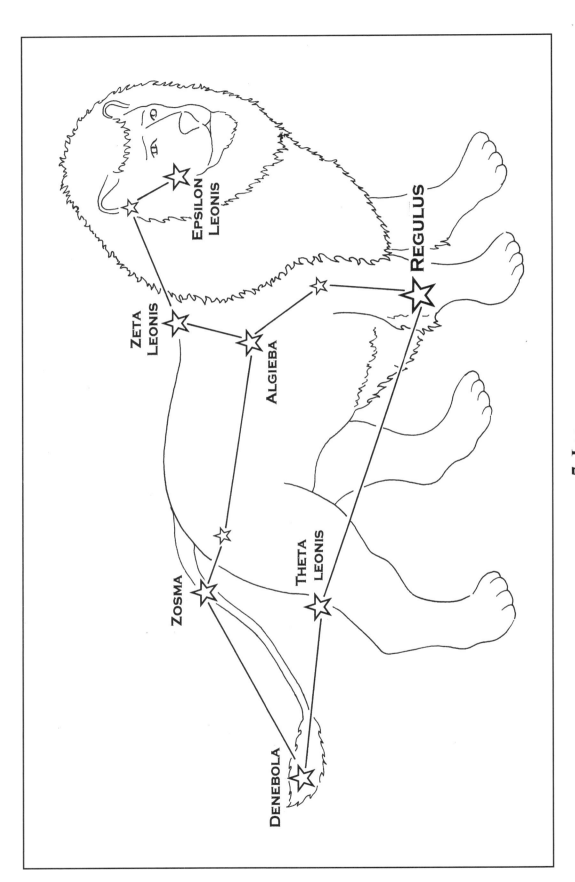

7. Leo
The Lion

Leo is also associated with the twelve labors of Hercules. Leo was named for the Nemean lion, a fierce and powerful animal whose thick hide was impervious to arrows and spears. Hercules wrestled the lion in a great battle and finally killed the beast with his bare hands. Hercules was thereafter usually depicted wearing the pelt of a lion. Those with birthdays from July 23 to August 22 are born under the sign of Leo.

The brightest star in Leo is Regulus (*Alpha Leonis*), located near the elbow of the lion. It is a blue-white star located seventy-seven light-years from Earth, with a magnitude of 1.35. Other major stars in Leo are Denebola, magnitude 2.1, Algieba, magnitude 2, and Zosma, magnitude 2.6.

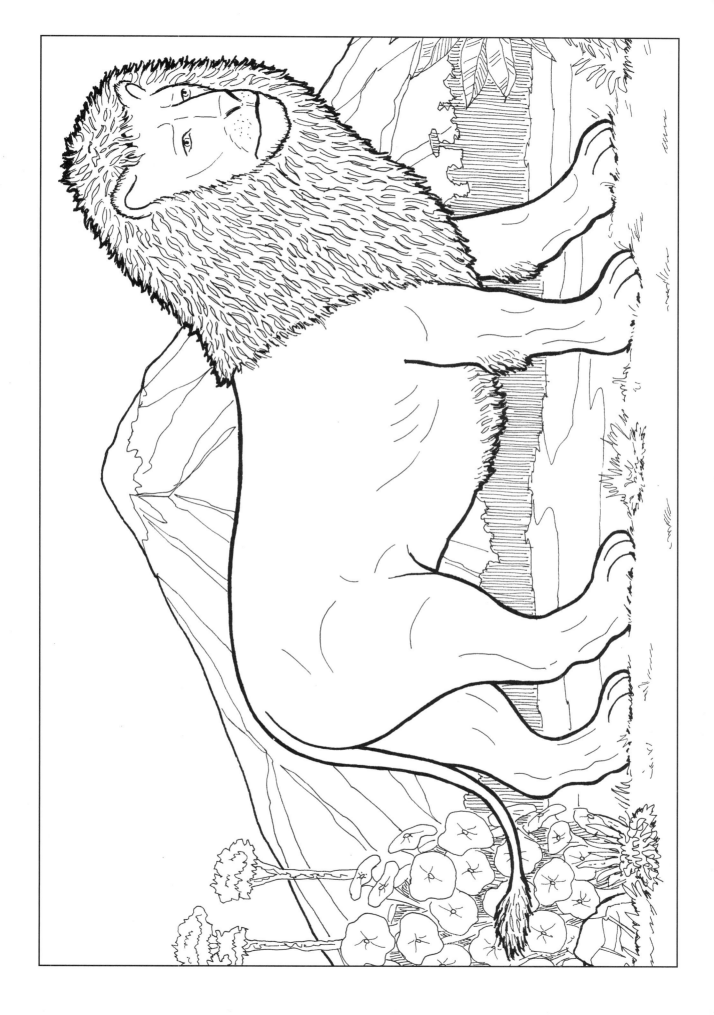

8. Virgo
The Virgin

The only zodiac constellation depicting a female figure, Virgo the virgin is based on a number of ancient myths. The figure has been said to represent the Babylonian fertility goddess Ishtar, the Roman goddess of justice Astraea, the Greek goddess of the harvest Ceres, as well as Ceres' daughter, Persephone, and the Roman Vestal Virgins of the goddess Vesta. Virgo is almost always shown holding a stalk of wheat, a traditional symbol of the harvest. The zodiac assigns the period from August 23 to September 22 to Virgo.

The constellation itself is the second largest in the night sky (after Hydra), and contains a number of interesting celestial features. Among these are the bright blue-white star Spica (*Alpha Virginis*), magnitude 1.0, and Porrima (*Gamma Virginis*) a binary star with a combined magnitude of 2.7. Also encompassed within Virgo are several star clusters and galaxies. The giant elliptical galaxy M87 contains over 200 billion stars while the nearby M104 Sombrero galaxy contains approximately 100 billion stars. These monumental star collections are both dwarfed, however, by the Virgo Cluster, a group of over 2,000 galaxies within the constellation Virgo.

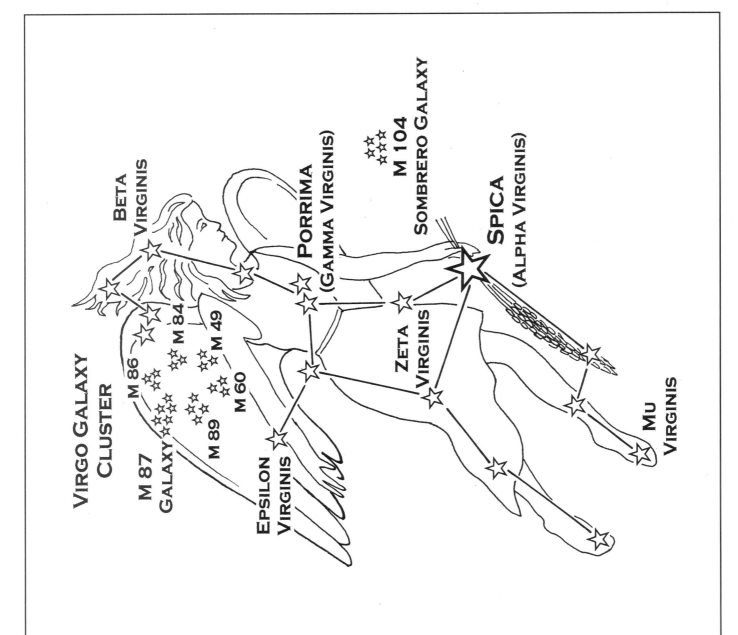

9. Libra
The Scales

Libra was originally included in the constellation of Scorpio. For this reason its two brightest stars *Alpha* and *Beta Librae* were called *Zuben El Genubi* (the southern claw of the scorpion) and *Zuben El Eschamali* (the northern claw) by ancient Arab astronomers. During the time of the Romans, Libra became a separate constellation symbolized by the scales of justice. Libra's zodiac time period runs from September 22 to October 22.

Alpha Librae is a double star with relative magnitudes of 2.8 and 5.2. *Beta Librae*, Libra's brightest star, has a magnitude of 2.6. *Delta Librae*, another binary star, has a magnitude which varies from 4.9 to 5.9.

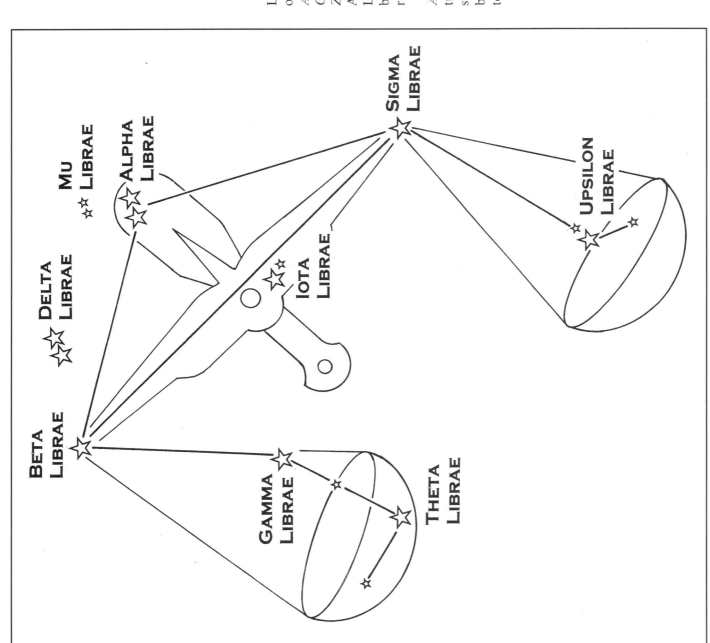

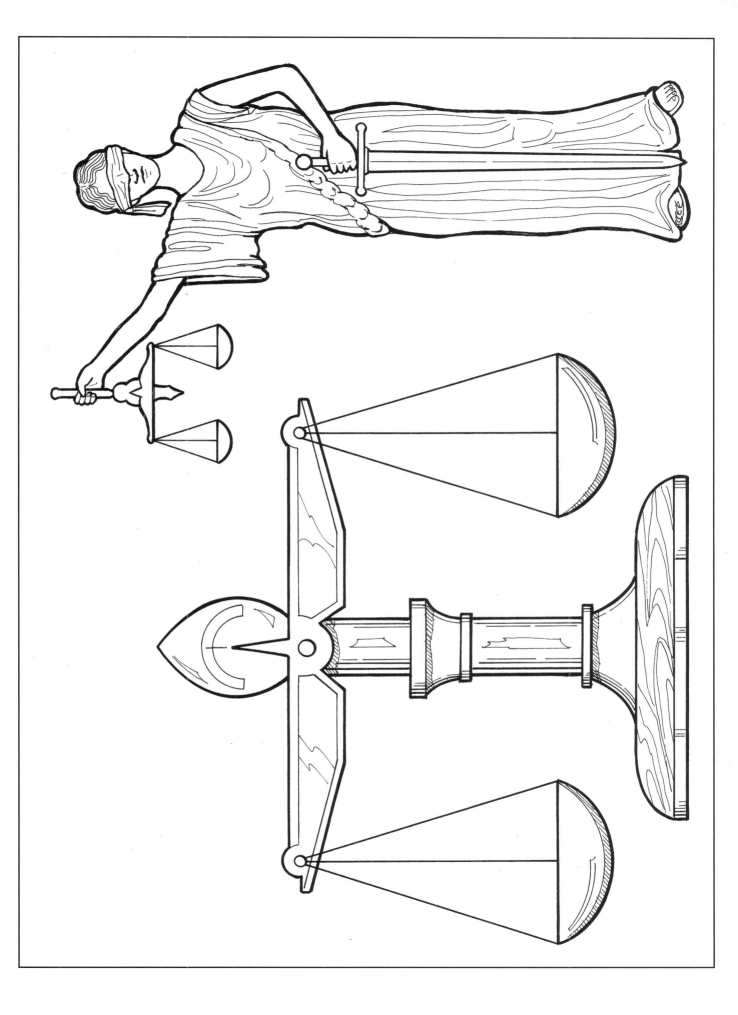

10. Scorpio
The Scorpion

One of the few constellations that actually resembles its symbolic image, Scorpio contains numerous stars and star clusters. They form a discernible head, pincers, body, and curved tail. In the Greek myth, Orion the Hunter is killed by a scorpion. Appropriately, the two constellations (Orion and Scorpio) are located at opposite ends of the night sky. Scorpio covers the time period from October 23 to November 21.

The brightest object in Scorpio is the red supergiant star Antares. The name means "rival of Mars," perhaps a reference to its red color. Its variable magnitude ranges from 0.9 to 1.2. Located at a distance of 345 light-years from Earth, Scorpio contains a number of double stars including *Beta Scorpii, Mu Scorpii,* and the multiple-star system of *Nu Scorpii.* Star clusters in this constellation include M4, M6 (The Butterfly Cluster), M7, and M62. These star-filled clusters lie thousands of light-years from our planet.

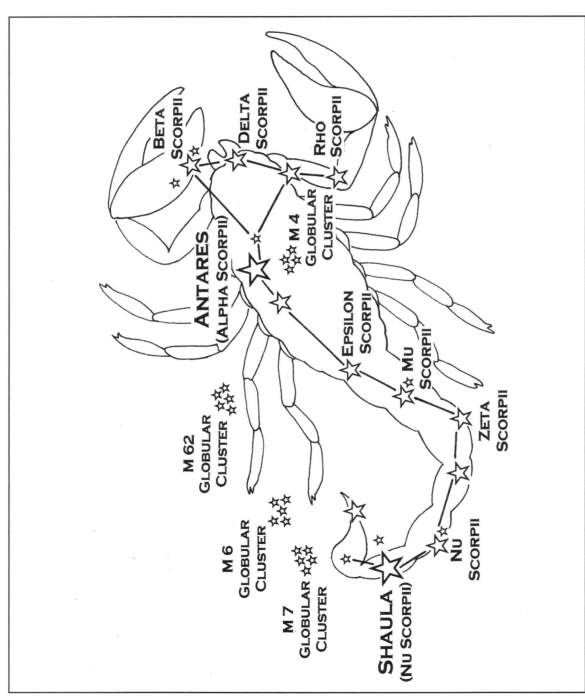

11. Sagittarius
The Archer

The constellation of Sagittarius is symbolized by a Centaur (half-man, half-horse) wielding a bow and arrow. There are several myths about Sagittarius. One states that the constellation depicts Crotus, the son of the god Pan, and an expert archer. Another identifies the figure as Chiron the centaur, who taught the Greeks medicine, music, and archery. The zodiac period for Sagittarius is from November 22 to December 21.

As you look toward Sagittarius, you are looking toward the center of our galaxy, the Milky Way. The most significant celestial object in Sagittarius is "the Teapot," a group of eight stars that form the shape of a teapot. The stars are *Gamma, Epsilon, Delta, Lambda, Phi, Zeta, Sigma,* and *Tau Sagittarii.* The constellation also contains the double stars *Beta* and *Nu Sagittarii* as well as numerous *nebulae,* clouds of gas and dust filled with newly born "protostars." Included are M17, the Omega Nebula; M8, the Lagoon Nebula; and M20, the Trifid Nebula, along with numerous other open star clusters.

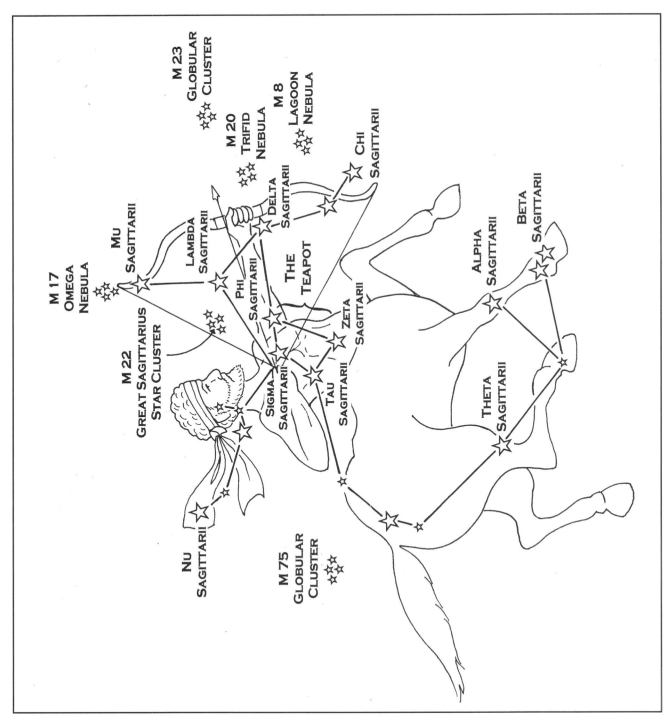

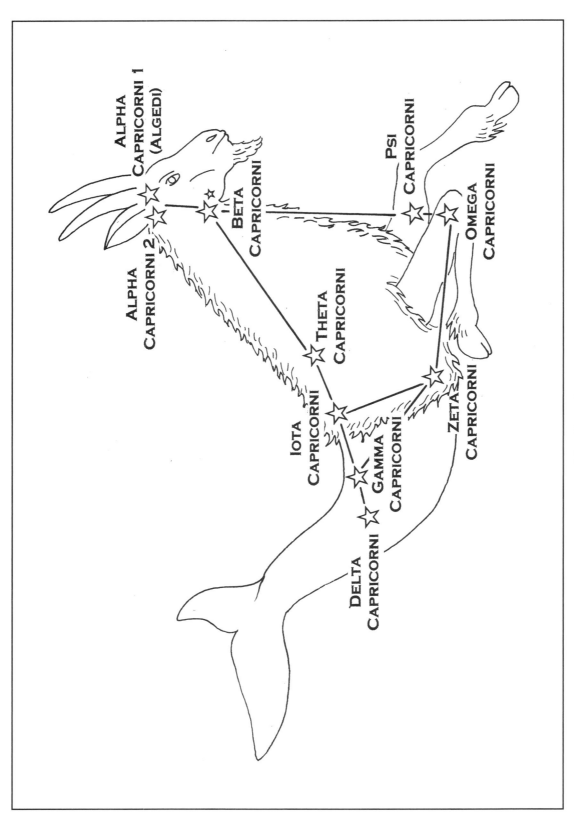

12. Capricorn
The Sea Goat

This constellation derives its name from the Greek myth relating how the god Pan, already half-man and half-goat, dived into the sea and turned his lower half into a fish in order to escape the monster Typhon. Those born under the sign of Capricorn have birthdays

There are no large or high-magnitude stars within Capricorn. It does contain the double star Algedi (*Alpha Capricorni*), located approximately 110 light-years from Earth. Another double star within the constellation is Dabih (*Beta Capricorni*), located 300 light-years

13. Canis Major
The Great Dog

The constellation of Canis Major has special significance for one important reason: it contains Sirius, the brightest star in the night sky. Sirius is a white supergiant with a brilliant magnitude of -1.46. Its brightness is also due to its close proximity to our world, only 8.6 light-years from Earth. Sirius is actually a binary star; its companion, a white dwarf star called the "pup," is barely visible due to the radiance of Sirius. Canis Major also includes another bright star, Adhara (*Epsilon Canis*) with a magnitude of 1.2. Other objects of interest within the constellation are the star clusters M41 and NGC2362.

The Great Dog is named for the hunting dogs of the legendary Greek hero Orion. Depicted in the illustration is an Irish wolfhound, the largest breed of dog. Fully grown, an Irish wolfhound can reach a height of 36 inches at the shoulders and weigh 160 pounds.

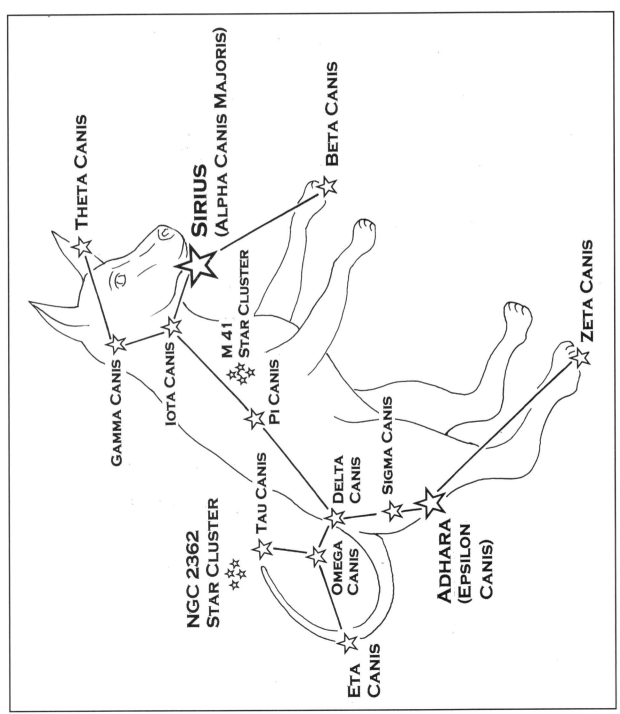

THETA CANIS

SIRIUS
(ALPHA CANIS MAJORIS)

BETA CANIS

GAMMA CANIS

IOTA CANIS

M 41
STAR CLUSTER

PI CANIS

ZETA CANIS

SIGMA CANIS

DELTA CANIS

TAU CANIS

NGC 2362
STAR CLUSTER

OMEGA CANIS

ADHARA
(EPSILON CANIS)

ETA CANIS

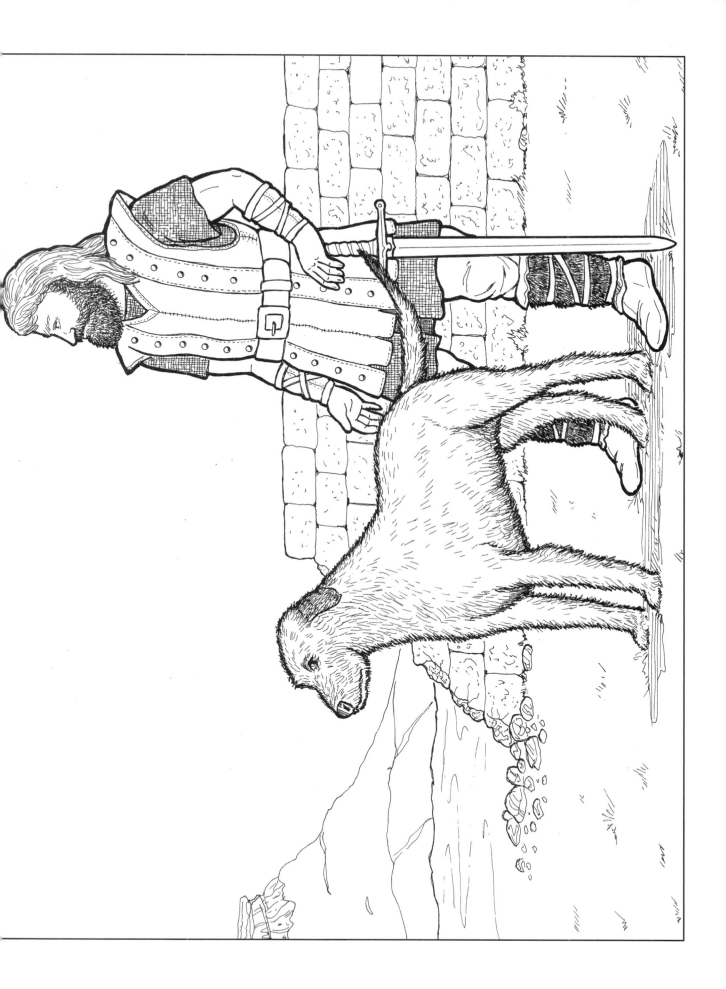

14. Orion
The Hunter

This constellation has been widely known and recognized by astronomers, travelers, and mariners for thousands of years. The ancient Chaldeans called it *Tammuz*, the Syrians named it *Al Jabbar* (the Giant), and the Egyptians, *Sahu*, son of the god Osiris. The Greek myth is based on the great hunter Orion, son of the sea god Poseidon. According to legend, Orion was slain by the sting of a scorpion. Fittingly, Orion sets in the night sky as the constellation Scorpio rises. Orion is most often depicted with the hide of a lion in one hand and a club in the other.

Orion is notable for several reasons. Primarily, it is distinguished by the fact that three of the brightest stars in the sky lie within the constellation. Most prominent is the blue supergiant star Rigel (*Beta Orionis*) with a brilliant magnitude of 0.12, the seventh brightest in the heavens. Next is *Alpha Orionis*, named Betelgeuse (pronounced beetlejuice), a red supergiant with a magnitude that varies from 0.3 to 1.3 every six years. The third brightest star in Orion is Bellatrix (*Gamma Orionis*) with a magnitude of 1.64. This constellation also contains the gigantic nebula M42, known as The Great Orion Nebula. This cloud of dust, gas, and newborn stars lies 1,500 light-years from Earth. The Horsehead Nebula, an unusually shaped dark gas cloud, is located near the three stars that mark Orion's belt.

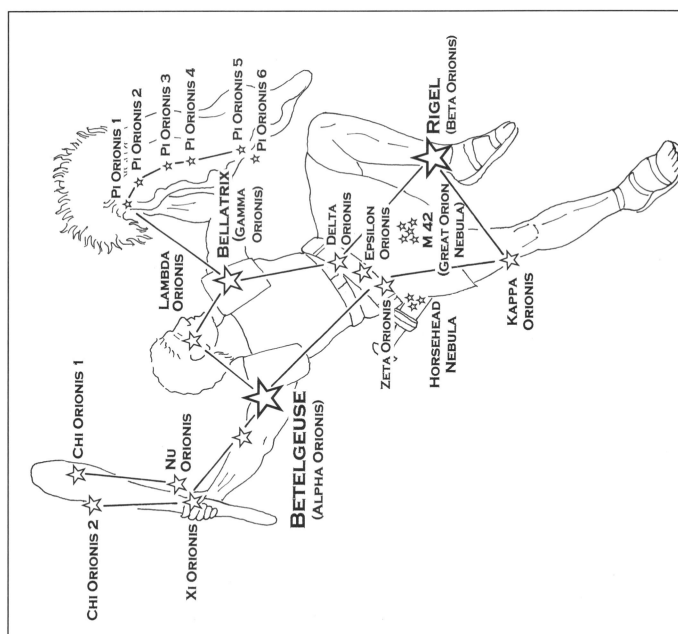

15. Aquila
The Eagle

The Eagle is marked by the star Altair, a white supergiant with a magnitude of 0.77, twelfth brightest in the night sky. In Greek mythology, the eagle carried the lightning bolts of the god Zeus, and also transported the youth Ganymede to Mt. Olympus to become Aquarius, cupbearer to the gods. Aquila also contains a Cepheid variable star, *Eta Aquilae*, a unique type of supergiant star whose magnitude fluctuates from 3.6 to 4.5 every seven days.

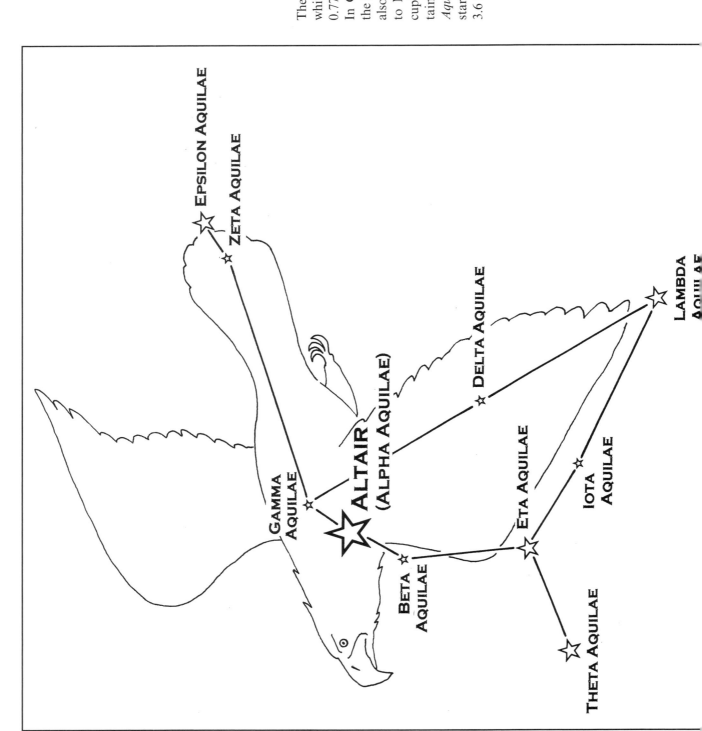

EPSILON AQUILAE

ZETA AQUILAE

DELTA AQUILAE

LAMBDA AQUILAE

GAMMA AQUILAE

ALTAIR (ALPHA AQUILAE)

ETA AQUILAE

IOTA AQUILAE

BETA AQUILAE

THETA AQUILAE

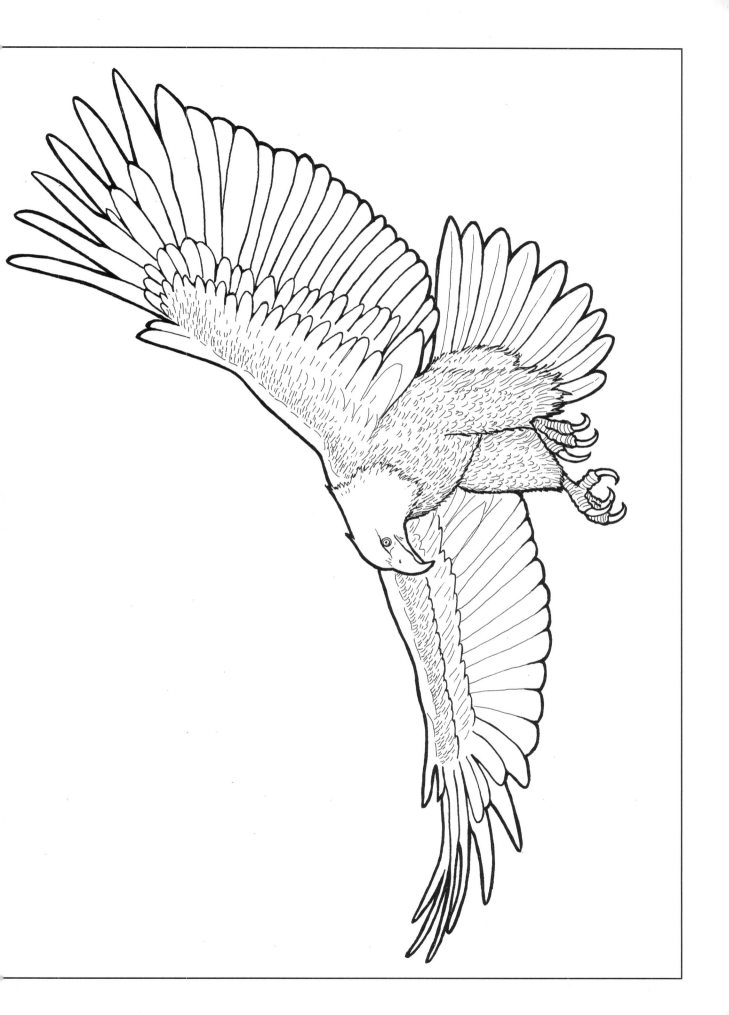

16. Andromeda
The Chained Princess

The story of Andromeda is one of the most famous ancient Greek myths. She was the daughter of Cepheus and Cassiopeia, King and Queen of Ethiopia. When Cassiopeia claimed to be more beautiful than the daughter of the sea god Poseidon, the angry god sent a sea monster, Cetus, to destroy the kingdom. The queen was told by an oracle that the only way to appease the sea god was to sacrifice Andromeda to Cetus. The princess was duly chained to a rock by the sea to await her cruel fate. Luckily, the hero Perseus arrived at the last minute astride his winged horse Pegasus. When Perseus displayed the severed head of the Medusa to Cetus, the monster was turned to stone and Andromeda was saved.

The constellation is especially notable because it contains M31, the Andromeda galaxy, the closest galaxy to our own Milky Way. A massive, elliptical, spiral galaxy containing over 200 billion stars, it is located 2.4 million light-years away from our home planet, a relatively short distance by galactic standards.

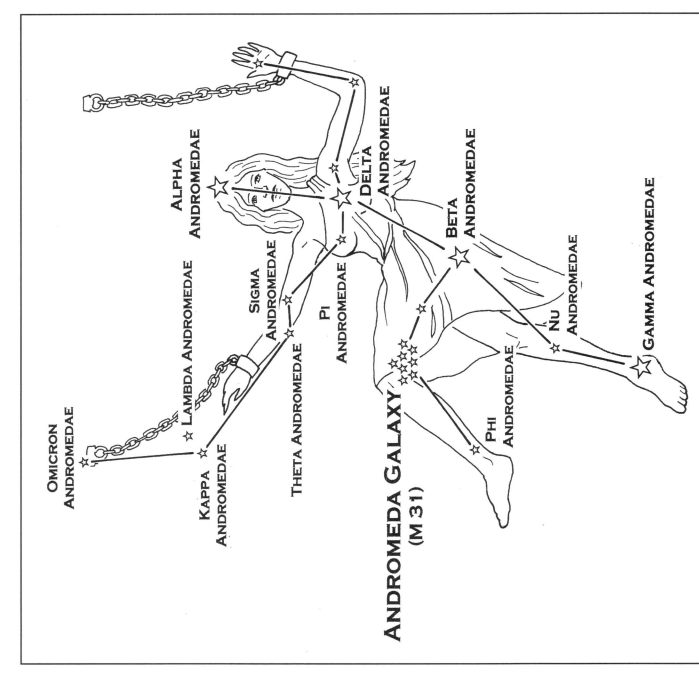

OMICRON ANDROMEDAE

KAPPA ANDROMEDAE

LAMBDA ANDROMEDAE

ALPHA ANDROMEDAE

SIGMA ANDROMEDAE

THETA ANDROMEDAE

PI ANDROMEDAE

DELTA ANDROMEDAE

BETA ANDROMEDAE

NU ANDROMEDAE

GAMMA ANDROMEDAE

PHI ANDROMEDAE

ANDROMEDA GALAXY (M 31)

17. Lyra
The Lyre

The constellation Lyra takes its name from the lyre, an ancient stringed instrument played by Orpheus, son of the Greek god Apollo. Orpheus was such a gifted musician that he could tame wild beasts with his playing. He was devoted to his beautiful wife Euridice (pronounced you-ri-di-chee). When she died, Orpheus descended to the underworld to save her. His pleas to Hades, god of the underworld, were so compelling that the god allowed Euridice to reenter the world of the living on the condition that Orpheus could not look upon her until they reached the surface. On the journey back, however, Orpheus was unable to resist gazing at his lovely wife and she was transported back to Hades forever. Upon the death of Orpheus, Zeus reunited the two lovers as stars in the night sky surrounding the lyre of Orpheus.

The constellation has many distinctive features including the blue-white giant star Vega (*Alpha Lyrae*). The fifth brightest star in the sky, Vega has a brilliant magnitude of 0.03. Lyra also contains numerous double stars, a quadruple star system, *Epsilon Lyrae*, and *R Lyrae*, a star with variable magnitude. In addition, Lyra contains the Ring Nebula, an unusual gas cloud so called for its resemblance to a smoke ring.

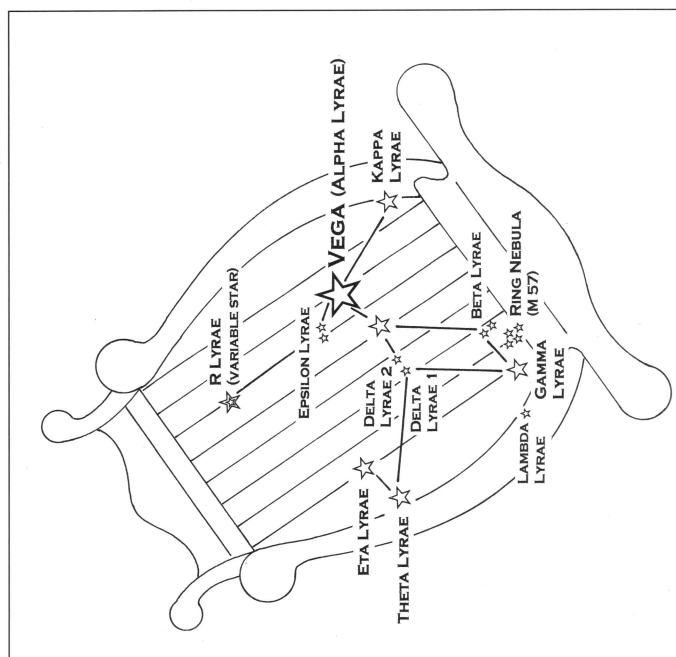

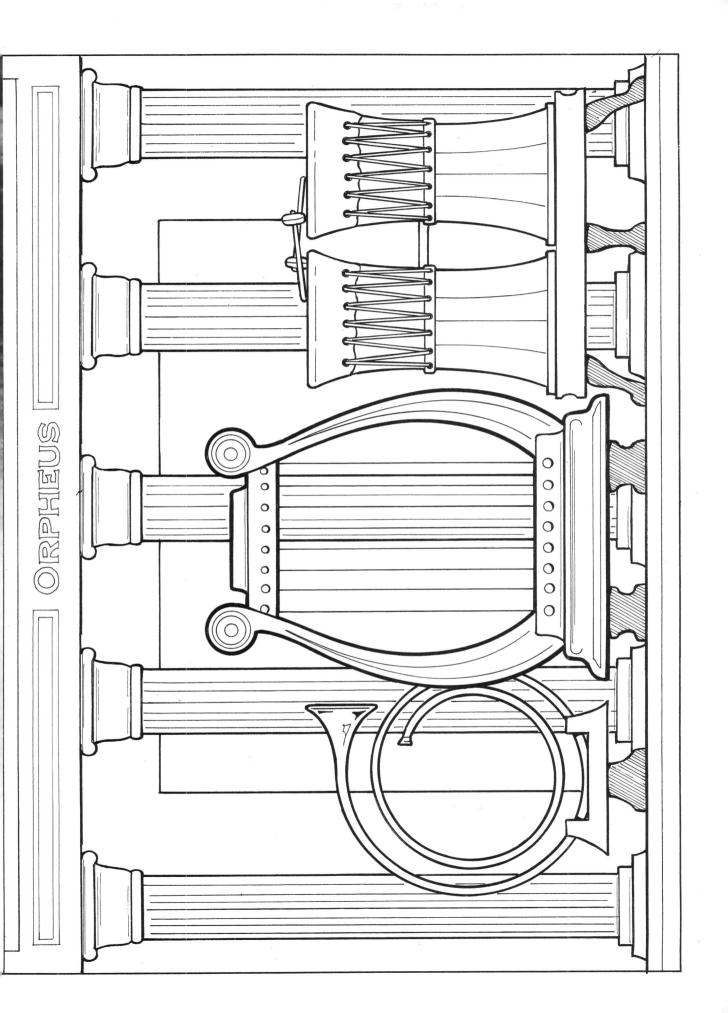

18. Ursa Major
The Great Bear (The Big Dipper)
and
Ursa Minor
The Lesser Bear (The Little Dipper)

These two companion constellations are perhaps the most famous and easily spotted star formations in the evening sky. *Ursa Major*, the Great Bear, or the Big Dipper as it is more widely known, is the third largest constellation in the sky. The handle of the dipper (or the bear's elongated tail) is anchored by the binary star Mizar (*Zeta Ursae Majoris*) and its companion Alcor (also *Zeta Ursae Majoris*). Mizar has a magnitude of 2.2, while Alcor shines less brightly at magnitude 4.0.

Ursa Minor, the Lesser Bear or Little Dipper, has been well known to sailors and other travelers for thousands of years. At the end of the mythical tail of the Little Bear (real bears have very short, almost imperceptible tails), lies the star Polaris, the North Star. So-called for the fact that it appears almost exactly over the North Pole of the Earth, it has long guided navigators by pointing the way to true North. The cup of the Little Dipper is formed by the stars Kochab (*Beta Ursae Minoris*) and Pherkad (*Gamma Ursae Minoris*).

The Greek legend of the Greater and Lesser Bears tells of Callisto, the mortal wife of Zeus, and her son Arcas. Out of jealous spite, the goddess Hera, wife of Zeus, turned Callisto into a bear. While hunting, Arcas almost killed the bear, not knowing it was Callisto. Zeus rescued both Callisto and Arcas by placing them in the heavens as companion constellations.

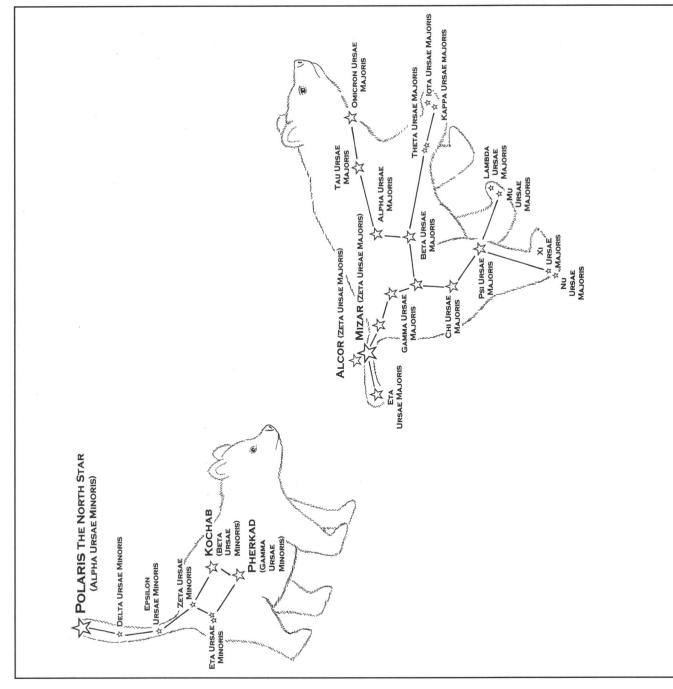

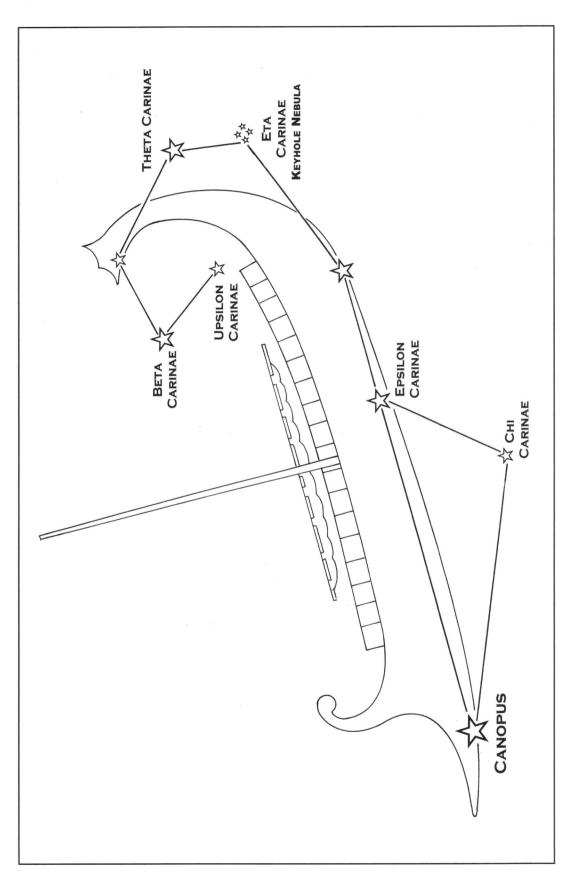

THETA CARINAE

ETA CARINAE
KEYHOLE NEBULA

BETA CARINAE

UPSILON CARINAE

EPSILON CARINAE

CHI CARINAE

CANOPUS

19. Carina

The Keel of the Great Ship Argo

This Southern Hemisphere constellation is located in a heavily star-filled part of the sky, making it a spectacular one to observe. It also contains the yellow-white supergiant star Canopus, the second brightest star after Sirius. Canopus shines with a beaming -0.72 magnitude. Carina also contains the Keyhole Nebula (NGC 3372), a glowing mass of gas and dust rently of the sixth magnitude, but has sometimes flared in the past to magnitude -1., second only to Sirius. Its mass and size are 100 times greater than our Sun, making it one of the largest stars ever discovered. In mythology, Carina is symbolized by the great ship Argo, which carried the hero Jason and his crew on their search for the Golden Fleece.

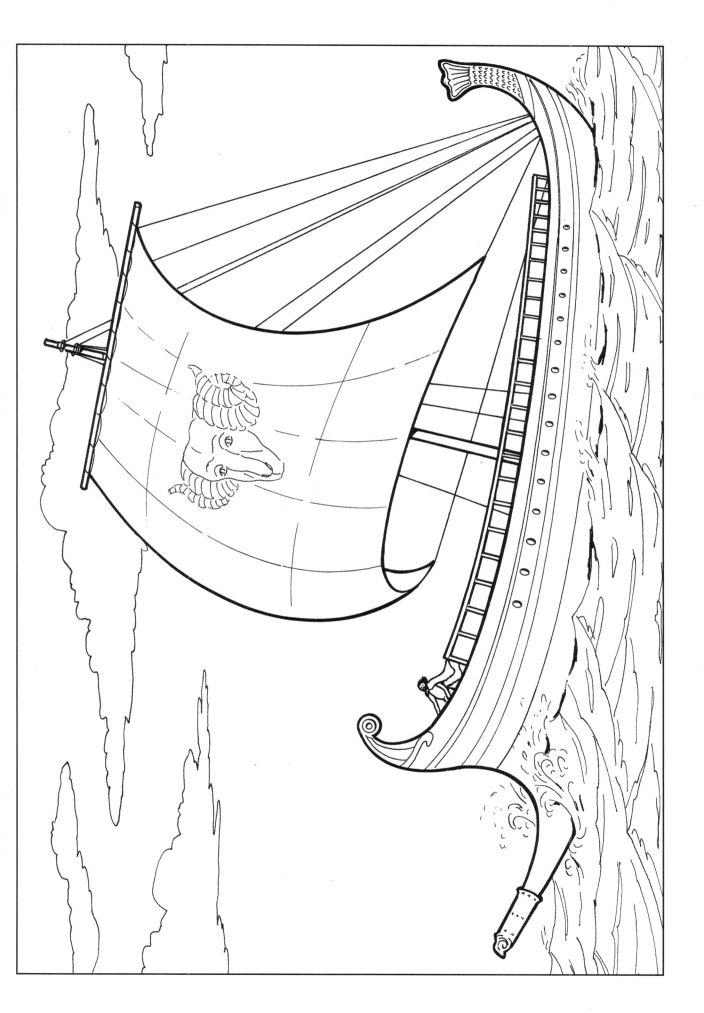

20. Centaurus
The Centaur

This constellation is represented by Chiron the centaur, a creature with the body and legs of a horse and the upper torso of a man. In legend, centaurs were often fierce and brutal, but Chiron was wise and friendly, eventually becoming teacher to many famous Greeks, including Hercules and Jason. The myth ends with the accidental injury of Chiron by Hercules. Because centaurs were immortal, Chiron, although in great pain, was unable to end his suffering through death. As an act of mercy, Zeus allowed Chiron to die and placed him in the heavens as a constellation of stars.

This large constellation is distinguished by the fact that it contains the binary star system Alpha Centauri, the closest stars to the Earth at a distance of just 4.3 light-years. Together, these two yellow-white type G stars shine with a magnitude of -0.01, third brightest in the dark night sky. A third much smaller companion, Proxima Centauri, was discovered in 1915. It is a red dwarf star only 40,000 miles across (by comparison, our Sun is 880,000 miles in diameter). Proxima Centauri actually lies at a distance of only 4.2 light-years, making it the closest star to our solar system.

21. Boötes
The Herdsman

The Greek myth concerning Boötes has several interesting variations and aspects. Given the name *herdsman*, one would naturally assume that Boötes was tending cattle, sheep, or goats. Instead, he is herding, or rather *guarding*, a bear. The name Arcturus actually means "bear guard" in Greek. One variation of the myth identifies Boötes as Arcas, son of Callisto and Zeus from the legend of Ursa Major and Minor. He is guarding his mother Callisto after she has been turned into a bear by the jealous goddess Hera. In another legend, Boötes is the son of Demeter, goddess of agriculture. For his crucial invention of the plow, Boötes was rewarded by Zeus with a place in the heavens.

The constellation of Boötes is distinguished by the very bright and nearby star, Arcturus. (*Alpha Boötis*). This yellow-orange giant has a magnitude of -0.04 and lies a relatively close thirty-seven light-years from Earth. It is the fourth brightest star in the evening sky. Boötes also contains a number of double stars including *Kappa Boötis, Mu Boötis, Eta Boötis,* and *Xi Boötis*.

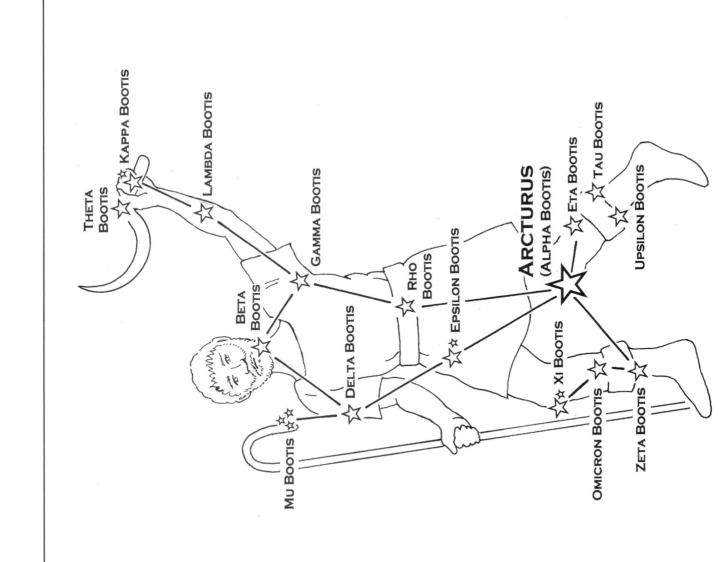

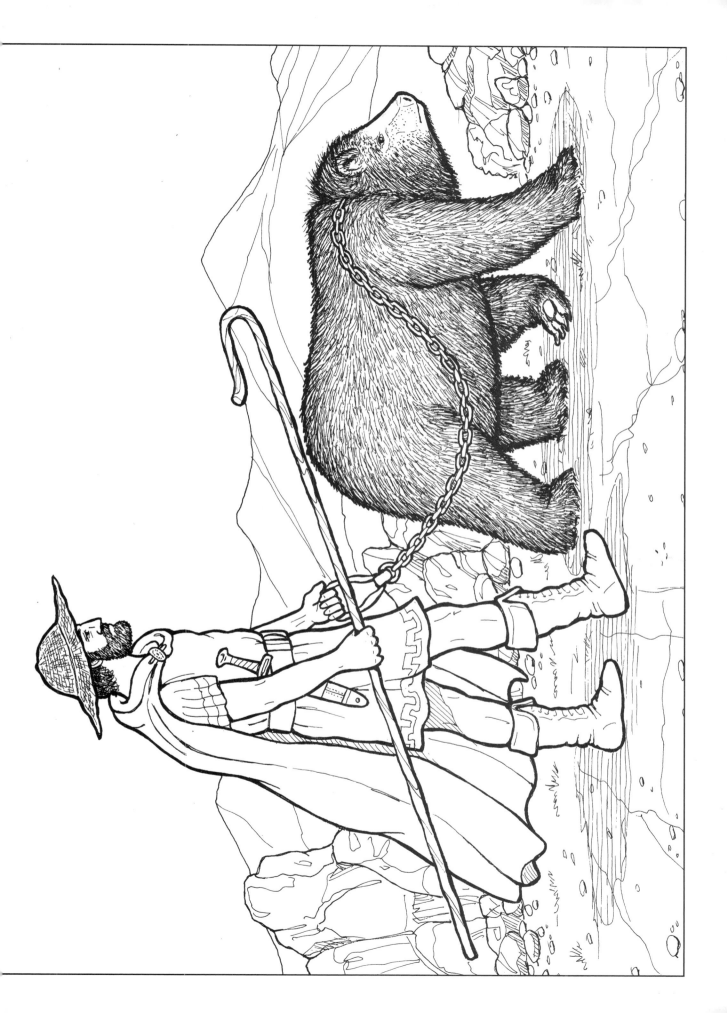

22. Perseus
The Hero

The legend of Perseus and Medusa is one of the most famous in Greek mythology. Perseus was the son of Zeus and the mortal woman Danae. The evil King Polydectes, while courting Danae, sent Perseus on a dangerous mission to try and get rid of him. Perseus was commanded to slay the evil Gorgon Medusa, a woman with snakes for hair, who turned men to stone when they looked at her. The hero was aided in his quest by the gods of Olympus. He was given the wings of Hermes and the brightly polished shield of Athena. Upon finding Medusa, he was able to cut off her head by looking at her reflection in his shield. When Medusa's blood dripped into the sea, it created the winged horse Pegasus. Perseus flew away on Pegasus to return home. While on his journey, he encountered the Princess Andromeda, chained to the rocks in sacrifice to the sea monster Cetus. Perseus rescued the Princess by exposing the severed head of the Medusa to the monster, turning it to stone.

The constellation itself contains the yellow-white supergiant star *Alpha Persei*. With a magnitude of 1.8, it is the brightest star in the constellation. Also within Perseus is the variable binary star Algol (*Beta Persei*). Its magnitude drops every two days from 2.1 to 3.4 as one of the pair of stars eclipses the other.

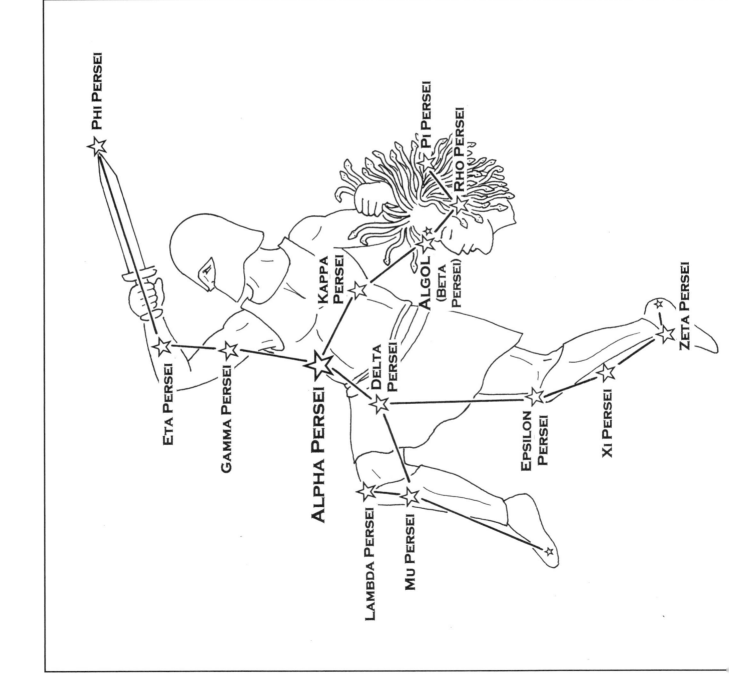